FOR LEFT HAND

(Eleven Melodious Studies for Piano)

by

John Thompson

(Book One)

ISBN 978-1-4950-3472-5

WILLIS MUSIC

EXCLUSIVELY DISTRIBUTED BY

Visit Hal Leonard Online at
www.halleonard.com

Contact us:
Hal Leonard
7777 West Bluemound Road
Milwaukee, WI 53213
Email: info@halleonard.com

In Europe, contact:
Hal Leonard Europe Limited
42 Wigmore Street
Marylebone, London, W1U 2RN
Email: info@halleonardeurope.com

In Australia, contact:
Hal Leonard Australia Pty. Ltd.
4 Lentara Court
Cheltenham, Victoria, 3192 Australia
Email: info@halleonard.com.au

FOREWORD

Studying pieces for Left Hand Alone provides more than just a "stunt" in piano playing. Of course, such pieces are novelties and as such, have a certain amount of merit. But they also contain values far beyond that of "trick piano playing".

First of all they provide much-needed additional training for the weaker hand—since most people are right-handed. Then too, left-hand technic is a very special kind of technic, requiring much jumping about to play the proper bass notes (very important) which usually occur under the weaker fingers (4th and 5th) of the left hand.

By giving one's entire attention to the left hand, strength and dexterity as well as accuracy can be immensely improved. Confidence is gained and the results are almost immediately apparent when, later on, both hands are used.

FINGERING

Fingering is a very vital part of all technic and this is particularly true when playing with one hand alone. Since there are only five fingers in use the selection of the proper fingering becomes of paramount importance. It is strongly recommended that the teacher be most insistant in the matter of using the exact fingering as marked.

TOUCH

Touch too, comes in for special development in one-handed playing since the melody tones as well as the accompanying figures must all be performed by the same hand.

USE OF THE PEDAL

The majority of pedal effects (especially in elementary music) are governed by the progressions in the bass. Thus it will be seen that music for the left hand alone provides a splendid exercise in synchronizing the movements of the left hand with those of the foot.

Of necessity, the pedal is used more in left hand pieces than in music written for two hands.

Every effort has been made to make the examples as musically interesting as possible to avoid the 'exercise' flavor.

When Book One has been completed, the pupil should be assigned Book Two which presents material in a slightly more advanced grade.

CONTENTS

Page

THE BEAUTIFUL BLUE DANUBE....................Johann Strauss   4

ELFIN DANCE..   6

THE SOUTHPAW..   7

ON PARADE..   8

MIDNIGHT BOOGIE..Jack Foy   9

ECHOES FROM SCHUBERT..   10

THE BALLET DANCER..   11

ON THE OLD BANJO..   12

FAREWELL TO THE PIANO..................Ludwig van Beethoven   14

MEDITATION   15

IN THE HALL OF THE MOUNTAIN KING..................Edvard Grieg   16

Here is a study in making wide skips between the melody and its accompanying chords. It is also a study in contrast between legato and staccato. Play the melody tones with your best possible singing legato and the chords with a light (shallow) touch. Use the pedal and fingering *exactly* as marked.

from
The Beautiful Blue Danube
(For left hand alone)

JOHANN STRAUSS

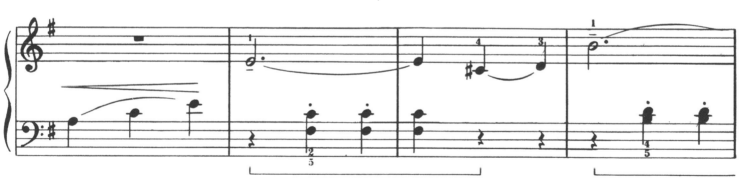

An example in three-note slurs. Be sure to use the fingers as marked and make a wide contrast between staccato and legato. Let the rendition be light and playful in the style of a *scherzino*.

Elfin Dance

(For left hand alone)

A study in legato scale playing, also in sustaining melody tones with the thumb while playing accompanying chords with the fifth finger side of the hand.

The Southpaw

(For left hand alone)

To be played in stirring March style. Sharp rhythm and strong accents. Be sure to catch the sustained notes in the bass with the pedal so that the hand can be released to move up for the chords in the treble.

On Parade
(For left hand alone)

A left hand arrangement of "Midnight Boogie" is included in this set of pieces by permission of the composer, Jack Foy. It is taken from his book, PRE-POPS — an extremely clever and 'catchy' collection of modern popular rhythms designed for 'Young America' in the first grade. (Published by the Willis Music Co.). Whether one approves or not, our youngsters are exposed to popular music and it is much better to learn how to read and understand pieces in this idiom — which, by the way, afford excellent study material in rhythm — than to attempt to play them haphazardly by ear.

The following example makes a fine exercise in passing the second finger over the thumb.

Midnight Boogie

(For left hand alone)

JACK FOY

The figure used here is taken from a famous song by Franz Schubert called, "THE EARL KING".
It makes an ideal study in passing the second finger over the thumb.
Be sure to make a distinction between the chords marked staccato followed by those bearing the sostenuto sign.

Echoes from Schubert

(For left hand alone)

In this example, the melody lies on the fifth finger side of the hand and must be sustained while the thumb side swings (using the 4th or 5th finger as a pivot) to play the light, staccato accompaniment chords in the treble.

The Ballet Dancer

(For left hand alone)

A study in light, bouncing wrist staccato. Try to imitate the sound of a banjo and play in humorous fashion.

On the Old Banjo

(For left hand alone)

This piece has been attributed to Beethoven although its real origin is in doubt. In any event, it provides a beautiful melody (on the thumb side of the hand) against a legato accompaniment. Frequently it is necessary to play several melody tones in succession with the thumb. This calls for very careful pedaling so as to preserve an even legato.

Farewell to the Piano

(For left hand alone)

L. VAN BEETHOVEN

In this piece the melody lies in the upper notes of the chords, played mostly by the thumb. Try to let most of the weight of the hand and arm rest on the thumb side as this supplies the 'pressure touch' so necessary in producing a singing tone. Be careful with the pedal.

Meditation

(For left hand alone)

Another staccato study. It is suggested that the staccato notes be played with wrist attack and the sostenuto notes with the forearm stroke. In measures 4 and 8 a choice of fingering is given. Use the one which feels most comfortable.

from
In the Hall of the Mountain King
"Peer Gynt" Suite

(For left hand alone)

EDVARD GRIEG